With love to my wife, whose infinite patience
and happiness keeps us all going.
- James Fogarty

First Edition October 2022

ISBN 978-1-7371089-5-5: Hardcover

ISBN 978-1-7371089-6-2: Paperback

ISBN 978-1-7371089-7-9: ebook

Clara and the Pink Unicorn

written by:
James Fogarty

illustrated by:
Mai S. Kemble

In the loftiest halls of lush verdant green,
Ruled a soft-spoken, sweet, and tulle-covered queen.

Her throne was a stump, sat on with care,
Florets as gemstones in golden blond hair.

Flowers - red, pink, and yellow – grew at her feet.
Blue ones, and purple, draped from her seat.

Majestically choosing each stalk, stem, and vine,
Crafting to show a new dessert divine.

Green leaves and petals to give it a start,
Layered with berries - some sweet, others tart.

Her creation set down, she browsed a new bunch
When from 'round the hedge came a crackly crunch.

She whirled quickly to see - startled of course -
And crept to the end to find out the source.

What slipped into view was a spiraling horn,
Rising sharp from the head of a pink unicorn!

Her mouth was wide open - it just couldn't be!
It sensed she was near and looked up to see.

The creature was lovely, huffed a glad-sounding noise.
It was wild and strong, yet it stood there with poise.

It sidled against her and lowered its head
And conveyed a clear message with no words being said.

Deep inside this queen felt the rise of a tide,
With a thrill, understanding, she'd been offered a ride!

But a nervous, bad feeling quickly pulled her apart.
It was a damp rankling chill, a fear deep in her heart.

She doubted herself! She hemmed and she hawed
While the creature awaited and patiently pawed.

But chances don't last, they'll eventually go,
Even if there's not a clear yes or clear no.

The moment was gone in a glittering rout
When across the back yard came a parental shout.

"Please watch where you step, and stay out of the plants!"

And - poof! - just like that -
gone was her chance.
It happened so fast,
there was no time for goodbye.
Her throat became tight
and she felt she would cry.

"But wait," she thought,
"We had such a connection!
I'll lure it right back with
another confection."

Blinking back salty tears,
feeling strength in her chest,
Determined to make what a
unicorn likes best.

She bunched up her skirts and
took off with a run.
With valiant new purpose,
this cake would be fun!

But while getting some leaves, serrated and thin,
Her shoe caught in a divot, and she tumbled in!

She rolled far too long - "Oh no, it's a hole!"
Then stopped face-to-face with an unseeing mole.

For being so small, to her he loomed large.
His tunnel - a canyon; his body - a barge.

The dimensions had changed - he was big, she was small!
Something like this shouldn't happen at all!

As the mole started nosing around to explore,
The queen spotted her shoe across the damp floor!

The mole scooped it up, he was running away!
"Oh stop it!" she cried, "Stop it, I say!"

Her face flushed pink and red, all in a huff.
Her favorite shoe! "I'll show you who's tough!"

There was no way she'd let him dig out of her sight.
She made a decision and focused her might.

Diving wide at the mole as he scraped through the cave.
To the mole- and herself- "I'll show you who's brave!"

She snagged back her shoe and raced up from the dirt,
With only a bit of her pride being hurt.

As she stumbled back into the light she adjusted
To scales that she knew, and perspectives she trusted.

In her shoe was a root - healthy unicorn feed!
She cried, "Oh my goodness, this is just what I need!"

She took some deep breaths
and pulled her shoe on;
Brushed back her hair,
and straightened chiffon.

A voice rang from the house
as she ran off with pep,

"Please don't get hurt, and just watch where you step."

She shouted, "Ok!" and
then took off again
And raced down the hill
to a neighboring fen.

Across a green log and
among the tall reeds
Stood some glistening
jewels disguised as bright
seeds.

She ran with intent,
cleared the log with a
hurdle, Nearly missing
the bottom of an upside
down turtle.

He rolled there morosely, looking quite at a loss,
His feet in the air, his head in the moss.

"Oh hello your majesty, I hope you are well!
It appears that I'm stuck in an upside down shell."

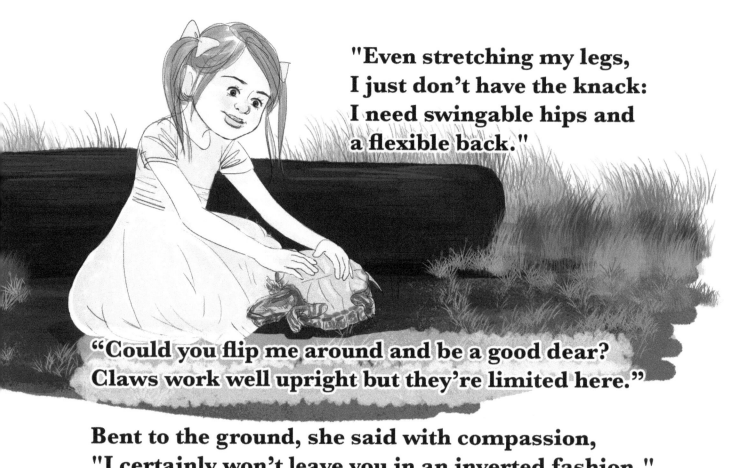

"Even stretching my legs,
I just don't have the knack:
I need swingable hips and
a flexible back."

"Could you flip me around and be a good dear?
Claws work well upright but they're limited here."

Bent to the ground, she said with compassion,
"I certainly won't leave you in an inverted fashion."

He helped with his kicks as she worked in the sun
Till he rolled with a thud, upright and all done!

He said, "One good turn, as you know, earns another.
Let me fetch you those jewels so you don't have to bother."

Happily back and forth shuffling out to the reeds,
He dropped in her hands those beautiful seeds.

"Thank you so much!" with surprise on her face,
She bowed and departed with wobbly grace.

She acknowledged requests to stay out of the dirt
As she kicked clean her shoes and brushed clean her skirt.

Now the cake only missed a unicorn topping.
Something rich and attractive - she knew just the thing!

Across the yard twisted raspberries tall,
Though spiderwebs closed this cavernous
sprawl.
 At the core of the webs leered 16
black eyes On a pair of black spiders of
enormous gross size.

A spider spoke up, "Now who do you suppose,
Is foolish enough to disturb our repose?"
The other replied, "Well, well! It's the queen!
Now this is a sight that we've never seen."

They crept on the webs, backs shiny as armor,
Baring fangs like long lances that could
certainly harm her.

Except for small gaps they were woven quite tight;
The queen reached her hand through the web on the right.

She gathered some berries as the sentries crept near.
Her hand shook more loose - now she rattled with fear.

The fruit tucked away, she rose up on her toes
To reach in once more for a hidden, red rose.

The first spider said, "If I weren't so full,
I'd make you regret what you're trying to pull."

The second chimed in, "But I'm not, my dear,
I've plenty of room, so there's SOME THING to fear."

The guard came in close, sneered, "Hope you don't mind,
I'm just going to check and see what you find."

"Oh no I don't mind, please just don't mind me,"
She said as she minded most terribly.

She grabbed at the bud, pulled it loose from the strands,
As she shook at the thought of 16 little hands.

But regardless of advances that seemed not quite nice,
Off came that rose, quite sharp and precise.

As she backed out, she then realized,
Fear had made them appear to her
oversized.

Now with these last pieces, a fine topping she'd make
For an alluring and tasty fresh unicorn cake.

Now for this dessert, the unicorn would appear.
The cake fully assembled, she withdrew but stayed near.

And return now it did!
The hooves treading light.

Her heart beat much louder,
with love and with fright.

No longer the queen of this boundless green world,
Now just an awed and trembling sweet girl.

The unicorn tasted its
well-crafted gift.
Content, it huffed once,
and again offered a lift.

Hesitate? "Not again!"
She was quickly astride
And holding on tight they
raced off for a ride.

Adventures they had and those without count
Till the last bump she felt was the final dismount.

She was back to her home, hugged the unicorn hard
As it nuzzled her back and trotted off in the yard.

Her regal persona was then set aside
As she raced to her family who was waiting inside.

She told tales of excitement, of places she'd roamed,
Though the best place by far was to be back at home.

As she played out the tale to kind, eager ears,
She felt growth in her heart past her actual years.

She glanced out the window when nearing the end
And saw prancing out there her lovely new friend.

She'd be out there soon, oh she knew that she would.
She'd travel the world now that she knew that she could.

Out there were adventures. There were friends to be made.
There were places to see. There were games to be played.

But right here and right now, where she'd take a rest,
Was her family and home; this, she loved best.

CPSIA information can be obtained
at www.ICGtesting.com
Printed in the USA
LVHW071942121122
733004LV00005B/110